THE
CANCER
ORACLE

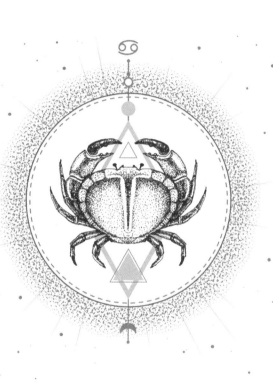

THE
CANCER
ORACLE

INSTANT ANSWERS FROM
YOUR COSMIC SELF

STELLA FONTAINE

greenfinch

Introduction

Welcome to your zodiac oracle,
carefully crafted especially for you
Cancer, and brimming with the wisdom
of the universe.

Is there a tricky-to-answer question niggling at you
and you need an answer?

Whenever you're unsure whether to say 'yes' or 'no',
whether to go back or to carry on, whether to trust
or to turn away, make some time for a personal
session with your very own oracle. Drawing on your
astrological profile, your zodiac oracle will guide
you in understanding, interpreting and answering
those burning questions that life throws your way.
Discovering your true path will become an
enlightening journey of self-actualization.

Humans have long cast their eyes heavenwards to seek answers from the universe. For millennia the sun, moon and stars have been our constant companions as they repeat their paths and patterns across the skies. We continue to turn to the cosmos for guidance, trusting in the deep and abiding wisdom of the universe as we strive for fulfilment, truth and understanding.

The most basic and familiar aspect of astrology draws on the twelve signs of the zodiac, each connected to a unique constellation as well as its own particular colours, numbers and characteristics. These twelve familiar signs are also known as the sun signs: Aries, Taurus, Gemini, Cancer, Leo, Virgo, Libra, Scorpio, Sagittarius, Capricorn, Aquarius and Pisces.

Aries   Taurus   Gemini   Cancer   Leo   Virgo

Libra   Scorpio   Sagittarius   Capricorn   Aquarius   Pisces

Each sign is associated with an element (fire, air, earth or water), and also carries a particular quality: cardinal (action-takers), fixed (steady and constant) and mutable (changeable and transformational). Beginning to understand these complex combinations, and to recognize the layered influences they bring to bear on your life, will unlock your own potential for personal insight, self-awareness and discovery.

In our data-flooded lives, now more than ever it can be difficult to know where to turn for guidance and advice. With your astrology oracle always by your side, navigating life's twists and turns will become a smoother, more mindful process. Harness the prescience of the stars and tune in to the resonance of your sun sign with this wisdom-packed guide that will lead you to greater self-knowledge and deeper confidence in the decisions you are making. Of course, not all questions are created equal; your unique character, your circumstances and the issues with which you find yourself confronted all add up to a conundrum unlike any other... but with your question in mind and your zodiac oracle in your hand, you're already halfway to the answer.

Cancer
JUNE 21 TO JULY 22

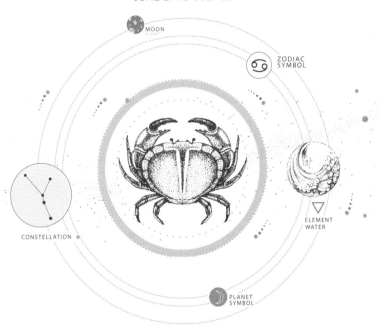

Element: Water

Quality: Cardinal

Named for the constellation: Cancer (the crab)

Ruled by: the Moon

Opposite: Capricorn

Characterized by: Imagination, empathy, tenacity

Colour: White

How to Use This Book

You can engage with your oracle whenever you need to but, for best results, create an atmosphere of calm and quiet, somewhere you will not be disturbed, making a place for yourself and your question to take priority. Whether this is a particular physical area you turn to in times of contemplation, or whether you need to fence off a dedicated space within yourself during your busy day, that all depends on you and your circumstances. Whichever you choose, it is essential that you actively put other thoughts and distractions to one side in order to concentrate upon the question you wish to answer.

Find a comfortable position, cradle this book lightly in your hands, close your eyes, centre yourself. Focus on the question you wish to ask. Set your intention gently and mindfully towards your desire to answer this question, to the exclusion of all other thoughts and mind-chatter. Allow all else to float softly away, as you remain quiet and still, gently watching the shape and form of the question you wish to address. Gently deepen and slow your breathing.

Tune in to the ancient resonance of your star sign, the vibrations of your surroundings, the beat of your heart and the flow of life and the universe moving in and around you. You are one with the universe.

Now simply press the book between your palms as you clearly and distinctly ask your question (whether aloud or in your head), then open it at any page. Open your eyes. Your advice will be revealed.

Read it carefully. Take your time turning this wisdom over in your mind, allowing your thoughts to surround it, to absorb it, flow with it, then to linger and settle where they will.

Remember, your oracle will not provide anything as blunt and brutal as a completely literal answer. That is not its role. Rather, you will be gently guided towards the truth you seek through your own consciousness, experience and understanding. And as a result, you will grow, learn and flourish.

Let's begin.

Close your eyes.

Hold the question you want
answered clearly in your mind.

Open your oracle to any page to
reveal your cosmic insight.

Return to nurturing your inner child if the world seems an unwelcoming place right now Cancer; coping can be difficult unless your resilience is in a good state of repair.

Challenging times call for strong self-awareness and understanding. Following the paths of others will simply lead you in circles Cancer – breathing life into your own confidence to increase self-reliance is vital.

Sure, you understand other people better than most, but that doesn't mean you never get it wrong now does it? Set your people-pleasing ways aside for this one Cancer, and focus on yourself.

True to your Cancerian nature,
your connections and understanding
are strong. This is a difficult one
though – you will need to offer
it up to the moon and
wait patiently.

Time to take a break from the
super-sensitivity; this tide will turn
(they always do).

You may feel that you are
seeing the world with fresh eyes
Cancer, suddenly party to new
information you didn't have before.
Take your time to re-adjust.

Of course, you are always quick to sniff out the truth. But sometimes you have to be patient and wait for it to find you in its own time.

Did you leap before you looked?
It might be that your certainty, which
usually serves you so well, was
misplaced this time. Try again.

It may not be the easiest idea
to get your careful Cancer head
around, but there are several potential
outcomes here (and you might
not be able to control them all).

Staying organized is important Cancer, especially if you want to maintain the flexibility to adjust your schedule at a moment's notice. After all, you can never tell when interesting but unexpected surprises will show up. Keeping on top of things will sharpen your response time.

Careful handling, as well as
your famous Cancerian intuition, is
usually enough to get you there all by
your amazingly resourceful self, but
this time you may need to
accept some help.

Make the most of your
ruling moon: see whether things
look different by night. Be open to
all possibilities.

You always consider others, of course; what self-respecting Cancerian doesn't? But that doesn't mean they operate in the same way you do – remember that.

When you know what it is you really want, there is nothing more powerful than that gut instinct Cancer is so famous for.

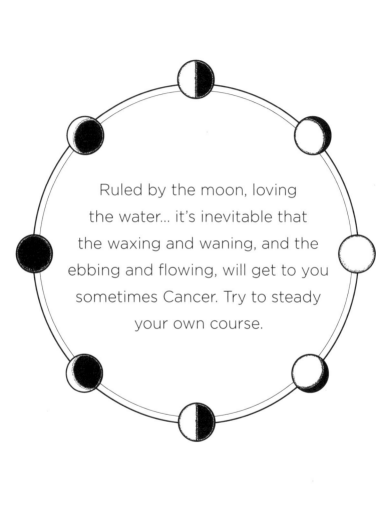

Ruled by the moon, loving the water... it's inevitable that the waxing and waning, and the ebbing and flowing, will get to you sometimes Cancer. Try to steady your own course.

Don't confuse your little rock
pool for the wide-open ocean. Less
scuttling, more stargazing.

Embrace your potential;
you don't always have to rely on
that tough exterior. Allow
everything to just be.

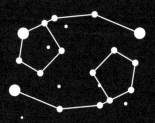

Try to take the long view on this one,
the world is wide open and waiting.

Change is a great idea and change-plans usually look good to you Cancer. But unless you are willing to take that leap of faith and actually put your plans into action you are wasting your time dreaming up these schemes.

You need to see this for what
it is, rather than trying to persuade
others to take your view. While half a
truth is not really the truth, half
a lie is still a lie.

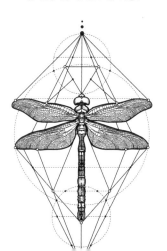

Congratulate yourself on
how far you have come, rather than
focusing on how much further
there is to go.

You don't always go with the flow;
sometimes it's worth remembering to
relax that grasp a little. Those things
that are meant for you will come your
way, but the ones you have to force
will never quite fit.

Remain loyal to yourself and commit to what matters – build up your own understanding and resources rather than relying on those of others.

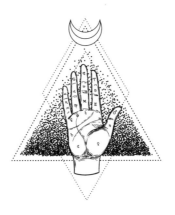

Your star sign has bestowed a rare emotional intelligence on you, but it is time to utilize your creativity as well. You will not achieve your full potential here without taking a risk.

A sequence of small wins
is the secret to success.

Great company, emotionally
savvy and easy to like, you've no
shortage of distraction opportunities.
Just don't make the mistake of
thinking everyone else will play
by your rules.

As a Cancer, using your gut instinct to get a handle on any problem is second nature to you. Your talent for recognizing the truth will serve you well again this time.

Cancers typically wear their
hearts on their sleeves, but not
everyone is able to reciprocate. Try
to remember that some people work
best if you leave a little more
space around them.

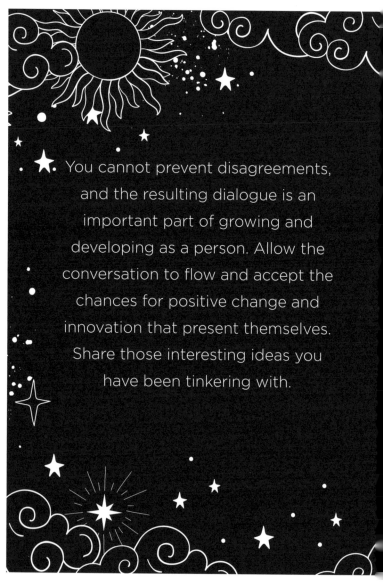

You cannot prevent disagreements, and the resulting dialogue is an important part of growing and developing as a person. Allow the conversation to flow and accept the chances for positive change and innovation that present themselves. Share those interesting ideas you have been tinkering with.

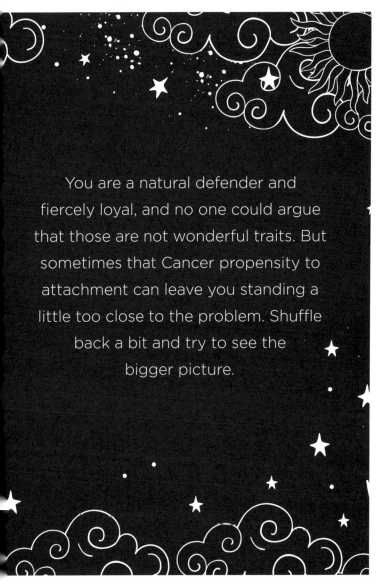

You are a natural defender and fiercely loyal, and no one could argue that those are not wonderful traits. But sometimes that Cancer propensity to attachment can leave you standing a little too close to the problem. Shuffle back a bit and try to see the bigger picture.

Wait, if you can, to see
what your moon brings you. Employ
patience, some deep breaths and
a little bit of trust.

Playing it safe doesn't sound particularly glamorous, but sometimes it is the best way. Don't push too hard or make too many assumptions. Wait and watch, and events will play out in their own way.

Relinquish your pincer grip
on what you think you want and wait
to see what the tides might wash your
way. You know they will turn.
They always do.

If there are important changes
you want to make but have been
delaying, now might be the time to
take those first few positive steps.
Feeling more in control, and seeing
others around you taking charge
of their own journeys, will be
both help and inspiration.
Do not delay any longer.

Remember, touching base with home (whatever that means for you) is the surest way to soothe frazzled Cancerian nerves.

Ruled by the moon, you have a strong instinct for self-care, and you love to create safe, nurturing spaces for both yourself and others to enjoy. It can be difficult for others to return the favour, because you are so often first to anticipate what might be required (and you do so perfectly).

Your true friend is the one who tells you what you *need* to hear, not what you *want* to hear.

It may not be the easiest path,
but your Cancer intuition is already
telling you that it will take you in the
direction you are destined to travel.

Daydreaming about the past or planning for the future are for another time; right now, it is important to be fully present.

Balance is key for you Cancer, and greater equalizing will mean better health and prosperity in all areas of your life. Confidence will flow and increased security will result.

Intoxicating though it is to
be asked your opinion, make sure you
have all the facts. Assume nothing.

Connection is a strong
Cancer skill, and one that brings you
enormous rewards as well. Make sure
you stay open to possibilities and
receptive to other people.

Turn to your friends for help maintaining that all-important good energy. Seeing off those bad vibes that have been knocking at the window lately is vital, never more so than now.

Interactions and relationships
that add stress to your life should be
avoided and allowed to simply run
their course and fade out Cancer.
Maintaining and nourishing them is not
only a waste of time, it is actively
destructive – especially so to one with
such an absorbent and intuitive
energy as yours. Don't let them
bring you down.

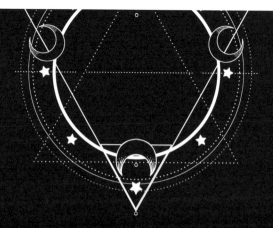

Don't play the victim;
it doesn't suit you one bit.

You have a strong instinct for warm people Cancer, and love to surround yourself with positive energy. Open yourself up to the possibility of stronger and longer connections with some of the interesting types you've crossed paths with recently – time to find out more about them and tell them more about you.

Imagining another path is a pleasing daydream and a fun way to engage with your creative brain. But if you are all dream and no do, you might as well spend your time more productively.

Different opinions can create conflict and your naturally harmonious nature tends to shy away from the harshness of it all. But it is important to stick by your ideas. Push yourself forwards, rather than retreating as is your habit, and take the time to explain your thoughts and the reasoning behind them. Further disagreement is possible, but the resulting conversation will be valuable.

Turn up for yourself, put your
best foot forwards and move.

Follow those leads Cancer,
there is a good chance they will take
you somewhere interesting.

As long as you suspend judgement and remain open-minded, those little seeds you have planted could very well take root and grow into something truly remarkable. Stand back and see what form they take.

Your nature makes you
one of the strongest zodiac signs
Cancer, and impacts every aspect of
your life. Both ambitious and dynamic,
while at the same time sensitive and
cautious, it is important to allow both
parts of yourself room to breathe.
Neither is better or worse than the
other – they just are.

Ruled by the moon, your energies
ebb and flow with an often regular and
predictable rhythm. When you feel the
drive to push into a more aggressive
mode, be mindful of the impact this
may have on those around you.

Scuttling around the edges
won't do much to increase your
prosperity Cancer; you need to stay
busy and engaged, present in the
centre of it all.

Sharing the emotional depths isn't everyone's comfort zone, even though it is the stuff of life to you intuitive Cancer crabs. Reassuring others that they can trust you only happens one way: proving you are trustworthy. Take this slowly.

Your network is a vital source of nourishment Cancer, both for its breadth and diversity, and for the support it provides you. Innovation and investment would be impossible without the support of all those holding you up; remember to send a bit of appreciation back in their direction every now and then.

Bringing your dreams to life will require action and fortitude; it's time to get to work. If you share your plans, there is a chance that others might be able to help you get there.

You can be a bit of a scuttler Cancer,
sometimes uncertain, and you may
feel out of sync with those around you.
This needn't slow you down though;
carry on regardless and you may even
hit your results a little earlier than
you originally planned.

Time to release some of that
pressure you keep piling onto yourself
Cancer. Mind, body and spirit could
benefit from an unstructured,
no-precise-outcome-required
rambling wander.

Diplomacy is a valuable skill,
and has its place of course, but don't
temper your words to spare other's
feelings when you are dealing with
someone wilfully causing unnecessary
grief. You have the power to step in
and the Cancerian intuition required
for quick understanding.

If people around you seem
receptive to your ideas, it's likely
they are making a place for you at the
table. Step forwards Cancer – you
have much to contribute.

Past friction does not always
rule out future compromise. If it feels
like something is shifting, flow
forwards into it, to embrace
the change.

With water as your element
Cancer, intuition flows freely with you.
But it can be exhausting checking in
on how you are feeling about things all
the time. Switch off the feeling faucet
for a short while at least and focus
instead on the practical.

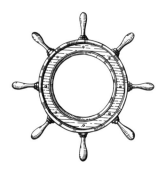

Connecting with others makes
you happy, and inspiration flows when
everything seems to line up in terms of
conversational give and take. Make
time to chat Cancer – dialogue holds
the answer you've been looking for.

Listening to that inner voice is vital Cancer – there's a lot of wisdom in there. Don't shut it down because you can't exactly explain it, or because it's 'just a feeling'. Intuition sits strongly with you.

Nurturing your self-understanding
is a lifetime's work; keep at it. The
road is not always smooth and
the rewards not always immediately
apparent, but the effort will pay
off and the results will
be transformational.

To such a self-sufficient sign,
others can often seem offputtingly
needy, desperate to be understood or
to form connections. Not everyone
has such a firm foundation in
self-awareness as you Cancer, and
your confidence is a gift.

Don't waste your time thinking
about potential consequences
Cancer, throw caution to the wind
and enjoy a little adventure.

With Capricorn sitting
across from you as your opposite
sign, you can draw on some goatish
hard-headedness of your own when
you need to. Although clashing isn't
really your style (you do, of course,
favour the sideways move), in this
kind of situation you need to
tackle things head-on.

Don't allow anyone (or anything)
to throw you off-course now you
finally know where you're heading;
no one else's journey will look
the same as yours.

A water sign, and ruled by
the moon, your energy flow and
the pull of the planets exert an even
stronger influence on you than they do
on most. The depth of your intuition
makes you feel almost psychic some
days. With all of this going on, be
aware that you need a firm
foundation, something
to anchor you.

Look out for ruby and pearl,
orchids and roses, and the colour
violet. These are all significant for a
Cancer, and if you are looking for a
sign, they may very well guide
you in the right direction.

Paying heed to your intuition right now may help you to avoid a particularly tricky obstacle Cancer. Focus on what's really important, rather than gathering too many conflicting pieces of information in the name of research.

Arguments with friends and those you love don't occur so frequently that you are oblivious to them, but neither do you always take them especially seriously. This time, you need to pay more attention – is the real point here something you might be missing?

Stay focused on what you need
to achieve right now Cancer. Ruled by
the moon and water, your attention is
sometimes pushed and pulled in
different directions. Concentration
is vital if you are to manage this
situation properly.

Not all obstacles require domination,
confrontation or the dreaded drama...
Perhaps you might simply crab-scuttle
around this one with your famously
graceful sidestep.

Are the issues under discussion the real problems here Cancer? Follow your intuition. Set your ego aside and hold the space open for what will come, and soon the truth will reveal itself or be shared. All in its own time.

If you are feeling vague or out-of-sorts, it might be a sign that this is not the best time for tackling very detailed, complicated, high-stakes tasks. Set your efforts to putting in some basic groundwork and preparation instead, so that you are all ready to move once your focus returns.

Rewards arrive in different
forms Cancer. Health, love, wellbeing,
contentment... you can't put them
in the bank, but you can invest in
and benefit from them
in countless ways.

This is the time to draw on that moon-gravity instinct of yours and find the best way to ask the right question. It will all be easy from there. The answer will reveal itself, right in front of you. Then all you have to do is go with it.

Connections are vital to you Cancer, but not always in a form that others instantly recognize. Your empathy and intuition run deep. The people who matter know that you understand a whole lot more than you often let on. The others don't matter at all.

Moving on is important, but so
is tying up loose ends as you go
Cancer. Find the beauty in the slightly
less-exciting tasks as well as the
more appealing ones – they are
all part of the balance.

Communication with companions, partners or workmates can sometimes take second place to actually getting the task done. This can be dangerous, particularly if people feel left out. Prioritize providing information to make sure everyone understands what is happening and why.

While the little details can
sometimes feel too fiddly and
complicated to spend your time on,
the big picture might equally prove
overwhelming. Just deal with the
sections you can cope with,
one by one.

Avoiding conflict is a very precise and particular Cancerian skill; you are easily able to extricate yourself from even the stickiest situation. However, others would do well to remember that those claws of yours can deliver a painful pinch if you are cornered.

A cardinal water sign, Cancer the crab is equally at home in the sea and on shore. The practical and emotional strength of your intelligence reflects this; draw on this balance to help you now.

Extremely sensitive, you crabs
use your tough exterior to guard
against hurt and injury. This shell might
cause others to regard you as distant,
perhaps even aloof. It might take
them a little while before they
understand you.

Massively intuitive and empathetic, Cancers will find being around negative or chaotic energy deeply draining, sometimes even distressing. Take care to guard yourself against too much contact with abrasive or manipulative characters – the damage they inflict may take a long while to repair.

Given how good you feel when you are on top of things Cancer, it is surprising how often you let the little things pile up into a have-to-do heap. Devote some time to organizing and clearing out – emotional, physical or both, it's all the same.

When welcome surprises come your way, be sure you take the time to both appreciate and enjoy them Cancer – that soft, under-shell bit of you should be both pleased and delighted.

Throw yourself into exploring
something new Cancer; it may
be tough trying to allocate time given
your schedule, but if you really want
to, you can find a spot for this
and later on you will be so
pleased you did.

When you are feeling the pressure of time (or, perhaps more accurately, the lack of it), take inspiration from how others are managing theirs. There is more than one way to get this done.

Don't let your task list become unwieldy Cancer. Devote small pockets of focused time to clearing the backlog, and you will feel freer in no time at all.

You never shy away from
emotional issues Cancer, in fact
quite the opposite: you embrace them.
Understanding the way others feel
about particular issues is the quickest
way for you to grasp the essence
of the whole person. Just don't forget
to play your part in the give and
take of this kind of sharing – it
has to be two-way.

Paying attention to those
who are giving you the gift of their
time is not simply good manners
Cancer, it is essential if you are to
garner the most value from these
precious interactions. Take nothing
for granted, and focus.

Dealing with new and
exciting opportunities is easy
for you clever Cancerians, because you
are so quick to read a situation and
your intuition gives you a clear steer
on the players involved. Don't let a
chance slide past you.

Self-care must be a priority Cancer;
put yourself first for a change.

You nurture your relationships
with uncommon attention and care,
but nevertheless conflicts occasionally
arise. Resist the temptation to wade in
and solve this one swiftly just so it's
done; watch and wait. A better
solution than you could have
crafted will result.

Actions will speak louder
than words in this situation Cancer;
much as you love a chat, now is not
the time to rely on your voice.
Roll up your sleeves and offer
some practical help.

Taking a step back to view
the big picture rather than getting
mired in the detail might be the only
way to achieve the best outcome for
everyone. Releasing your hold may
feel risky, but you need to leave the
smaller points to others and go with it.

Of course you prefer to stick
to the safe questions... who doesn't?
But are you sure this question is really
the one you want to answer right
now? Try again Cancer.

Harmony in all things; your intuition unfailingly guides you in the direction of peace Cancer. Scuttling away from conflict is one of your keenest instincts; run with it now.

Companionship works for Cancers, but only if it flows naturally and certainly not if it is taking a negative toll on your energy. Don't forget to support yourself as well as those around you. Harmony should be more compromise, less cost.

When you know what it is you
really want, there is nothing more
powerful than that determined focus
Cancers are so famous for.

Gentle, instinctive, tactile and
kind – Cancer really is an irresistible
sign to many. The ability to draw
others towards you is a gift, and
one you should make the
most of right now.

Your talents are numerous and
when you apply yourself there's plenty
you can handle. Do not underestimate
yourself Cancer. Just remember, some
people might take a little longer
to win over than others.

You are known for your strong intuition and the care and thought you extend to others. But when expert help is required, ask. It is important that you take advice where you need it, you can't possibly do this all by yourself.

Suspend judgement until
you have heard the whole story;
do not underestimate the value of
patience here – you will understand
more later on.

You are not used to being
the expert in the room Cancer, so it
can be intoxicating and exciting when
people specifically request your
opinion. Be sure you are giving them a
clear and thoughtful response, rather
than becoming swept up in the
excitement of it all.

Take care that your self-confidence
does not swell into an unpleasant
and unappealing sense of entitlement.
Consider the feelings and the rights
of others, and nip this in the bud.

Tact is one of your particular strengths, as is watchfulness and an ability to make others feel good about themselves. But it is important to maintain your true connections and to reinforce your relationships with those who truly matter to you – watching you work the room might leave them feeling doubtful about whether they really hold a special place in your heart. Reassure them.

Others may find fault with your carefully mapped-out plan... and perhaps they are right? It might be that you did not give this one the full level of consideration it merits. Only you know the truth here.

The moon brings emotion and
sensitivity to the surface in all you do
Cancer, and it also encourages great
beauty and strong intuition. Your keen
awareness of the world around you
is both a blessing and a burden –
resist absorbing too much
lest it weigh you down.

When you pressure yourself
to succeed, usually it works.
Self-motivation is important for
you Cancer, prone as you are to
drifting. This one is tricky but
persevere and you should be
able to get it done.

It's time to show yourself some love Cancer. Turn that kindness, which you so generously bestow on those around you, inwards for once.

Patience, Cancer. Light, caring and intuitive as you are, you are not omnipotent. There is still something you need to know, and waiting is the only thing to do right now.

Adopt a neutral stance on this one
Cancer. It is not your battle to fight.

This is a tricky one and the details are not as they seemed at first glance. Take a closer look – there is nuance there that was not apparent to start with.

Find the way back to your truest
self Cancer. Love is the answer.

An issue you are playing around
with in your mind right now will need
more rumination. If you're still not sure
where to turn, ask a friend or
colleague for some time and talk
things through with them.

Have faith in your star-path and relinquish that crab-pincer control grip. You do not need to have all the answers prepared. Allow yourself to bob along with the tides for a while now.

Remain open to the possibilities
that lie ahead Cancer; endeavour to
stay quietly aware and prepared for
whatever the universe will bring.
Change is on your horizon but
be assured that there is nothing
you can do to plan for it.

Follow your heart, rather
than your less pure motivations, and
the rest will fall into place.

The success you have dreamed of and worked so hard for is on its way, although it might look slightly less spectacular than you had imagined. A series of small wins is the key to this one, celebrate each and every one.

Lean into your intuition this time and keep your opinions to yourself. You've learnt this lesson before but giving advice will shackle you to an outcome – and really, this is not your game.

With Capricorn as your opposite
sign, sometimes you need to dig those
heels in and engage with a little more
determination and stubbornness. Now
is one of those times you really do
need to Be More Goat. Only you
can do this for yourself.

Patience and persistence
will be key this time. You are good at
both of those. Bide your time.

Throw that fine-tuned Cancer intuition into high gear; possibility is more complex and resonates infinitely more deeply than what you can sense on the surface.

If you are feeling left behind or bewildered by the ebb and flow of power dynamics at the moment, you are likely not alone in this. It's just that your soulful sign finds manipulation and jostling for position a little more difficult to justify than most. Hold tight to your own beliefs Cancer.

The whisper of something difficult from your past might leave you feeling a little haunted or even slightly spooked Cancer. Simply sidestep this and don't give it extra life by letting it burrow under your shell.

A good friend will hold a space for you to come to the truth in your own time, with love and patience. Acknowledge the loyalty of those who stand quietly beside you – they bring real love.

Cancer, you know that you will
only keep bringing your best game
if you allow your energy to replenish.
Embrace some downtime today
and you'll be ready for action
again soon.

Your seemingly effortless
Cancer gift for understanding
others will ensure you are easily able
to fix your focus on the task at hand.
A more comprehensive understanding
will simplify your approach, but you
must apply yourself properly. Resist
the lure of sparkly distractions.

Look carefully but without judgement Cancer; this is a particular gift of yours and one you should make good use of right now.

Forgive the mistakes that
have been made, whether by you
or by someone else. Forgiving doesn't
mean forgetting but moving on with
your own life is the only reasonable
course of action.

The moon parades a circus of emotions through you, almost on a daily basis, and learning to live easily with these constant companions takes work. Understand that your happiness is a necessity, not a luxury. Proceed accordingly.

Gentle as you are, you also
love a challenge. Nothing worth doing
seems easy at first, but you are more
than up to this one. Just resist the
urge to obsess over it – you cannot
allow yourself to be defined by
success or failure.

Trust your instincts Cancer.
Your first impulse was the right
one – now is not the time for second-
guessing. Steady your hand, set your
course and go for it.

Adversity often brings opportunity, but sometimes it can all feel too much and you would rather give up. Try to take the long view and see past the immediate issue to what likely lies ahead. You don't need to plan every step along the way to get there.

It is likely that this will not be the
easiest journey, but you seem to have
your bags already packed. Understand
that difficulties will arise and you will
deal with them and continue onwards.
Once you have embarked on this
(and in your heart you already have),
giving up will not be an option.

Providing nurturing need not be your inevitable role Cancer. Make a choice this time to put your own needs first and watch how well it turns out. This situation may prove to be a revelation and a turning point in one!

Set some boundaries and establish the way you want to function moving forwards. Everyone will work better for being clear about this.

Empty words and hollow
promises are not the way you play.
You are what you do Cancer. Don't
be tempted to sidestep integrity –
it has carried you this far and
served you well.

You have weathered enough
storms to ensure that quiet self-belief
is in steady supply for you Cancer.
Your honest, pragmatic approach
won't let you down. You have the deep
knowledge already within you to make
the right choice.

Do not be swayed by flattery
or attempts to drop a rosy filter
over the truth; you know what
you know Cancer.

Adjust your approach... there is a chance your first move might have been a step in the wrong direction. Best to recalibrate your compass now, before you have travelled too far, and view this as a chance to learn and move forwards (the right way this time!).

Being excited is one thing,
playing to the crowd is another.
Be true to yourself Cancer – if your
reaction doesn't satisfy them, that
says more about them than you.

The hard work stuff can be a bit of a drag sometimes, but it doesn't need to be if you just re-frame your thinking slightly. Make sure this one doesn't end up being so predictable that you (or they) lose interest. Breathe a bit of oxygen into it. Add some spark.

Giving yourself credit for your successes, whether big or small, is vital for keeping everything in balance. Straining to succeed is no good if you don't acknowledge your own achievement. Time to test your flexibility and pat yourself on the back.

Letting go doesn't have to be
the same as admitting defeat –
sometimes the biggest win is in
freeing yourself from the struggle.
If things are meant to work themselves
out, they will.

Having fun is on the cards
for you Cancer; just remember that
you will need to take absolute
responsibility for your own actions
(sorry if that doesn't sound *quite* as
enjoyable now...).

Despite your heart's keenest longing, it will not be possible for you to control this outcome Cancer. Make the cleanest decision you can, for the part that you are able to influence, then retreat. Watch and wait if you must, but if you can turn your back altogether then all the better.

Soothe your water-loving soul in the sea, in freshwater lakes or rivers, or even in long luxurious baths Cancer – placate your inner crab and turn off your thinking brain for a while.

Different results will signal success to different people. In this situation, understanding the outcome may not be clear cut. But that's not important.

Leave your chess-game strategy
at the door today; decide which way
you want to scuttle and get moving.

A finely balanced solution
is particularly satisfying to a Cancer;
weigh it all up carefully before
making a call.

Smugness and satisfaction:
there can be a fine line, but it is
easily navigated by your innate
self-awareness Cancer. Celebrating
your achievements is important.

Your propensity to sideways
glances and your strong intuition
mean you are very rarely taken
off-guard; you usually know the lie of
the land long before anyone else does.
Prepare yourself for what's coming –
you've a pretty clear idea of
what it will be.

It may have taken you longer than most to think things through and finally decide what you want. But now you're clear, your Cancer focus gives you an excellent chance of success. Time to make it happen.

Events ebb and flow like the waves Cancer, and often there is little you can do to maintain balance. It can feel particularly disorienting when things keep tumbling in and out on top of each other. Trust that there is a greater plan at work right now. Breathe, stay in the moment, relax your grip on that you are seeking to hold and this too shall pass.

A clean slate and a fresh
start are vitally important now
Cancer. You know there is a better way
to go about this, despite the fact it
may seem a slightly more difficult path
from this angle. Don't allow yourself
to be disheartened.

Cancer is a water sign; go
with the tides right now, rest easy
in the confidence that the waves will
bring you back to the place you are
meant to be.

This is far from an impossible one for you Cancer. But you might need to look at the situation from a different angle. Your direction of approach will make all the difference to your chances of success.

That silver light of your ruler, the moon, bathes everything previously familiar in a new liquid coating. By the same token, you see things differently to other people Cancer, and that's just the way it is. This is second nature to you but might be a puzzle to others.

You may require some assistance
with this one Cancer... luckily your ego
rarely overrides a practical approach,
so you should have no problem
asking your tribe for help.

Escape to the water while you
think this through Cancer – you need
plenty of flow moving around you
right now to avoid getting stuck.

Your hard-working protective shell
keeps all that is soft safe inside. Do not
let the irritating or irrational, or those
who would harm you, find their way in
beneath the surface – the resulting
hurt will not be worth it. Stay alert
and guard yourself.

Your gut instinct was, of course, correct. Isn't it always? Follow that famous Cancer intuition again on this one; it will not set you wrong.

Plenty of people have opinions about the way you should do things, and for some inexplicable reason they just love to let you know... Don't be tempted to do this anyone else's way Cancer. You know what's right for you.

The decision to aim for a system-shaking change is rarely well-made when it is taken as a knee-jerk reaction. Sleep on it.

Extreme rationality simply doesn't resonate with you Cancer. When it comes to it, how a person or situation makes you feel is pretty much everything. Allow yourself to truly understand this, then make your decision accordingly.

Determined and responsible
when it comes to your duties, you
are the one others turn to for the
important things. Be clear about the
environment and engagement (or lack
thereof) necessary to create the most
effective, conducive situation.

The Cancer crab is a sensitive
and gentle creature, but you really
love to bask in approval when it comes
your way. Stay realistic and be wary of
this tendency tipping over into
something darker or hungrier. It's not
your style. Reassure yourself: you are
all that you need to be. You are
already enough.

Your people trust you, and you have fun with them, but you have a tricky knack for keeping most of them at pincers-length. It's a hard one to explain. Remember to prioritize your loved ones and invest a little more warmth in your relationships.

Sometimes it is possible to assess and evaluate your own experience and emotions with clarity and detachment, without getting swept into the feelings-whirlpool of it all. Such days are a gift and will allow you to make some great progress. Do not be so careless as to dismiss or fail to take full advantage of them.

Be careful that your words
and thoughts don't tie you into
knots Cancer – over-thinking this one
will likely just serve to trip you up.
What's more, it's not really in your
nature. Do not sink too much of your
precious time into this.

Resist second-guessing
yourself Cancer, instead you
should trust your silvery moon-guided
intuition. Open your heart, that you
might understand what it is telling you
more clearly. Let it guide you.

Light and clarity may be flooding
in at the moment Cancer, leaving you
blinking and a little bewildered by
recent events. Take your time getting
used to the way things look now.

The more active you are, the
more capable you will be at handling
any dramas and obstacles that career
along life's highway towards you.
Push yourself a little harder than
usual and keep that oxygen
moving through.

Your honesty and integrity
have brought you further than
you might think Cancer, especially in
terms of the level of respect and trust
others have for you. Different people
might be more inclined to grab the
limelight and revel in the applause;
you mustn't feel resentment towards
them. That isn't your way.

Dark and light maintain a
delicate balance with you, Cancer.
Ruled by water and the moon, it can
be tempting to slip into the shadows
slightly more often than perhaps is
helpful. Make sure you can be seen
right now, others need to know
that you are there.

Walking or being near the water,
or best of all both, will give you the
creativity surge you need to craft
a clear, focused and effective
solution to this one Cancer.

Maintain your focus on substance and integrity Cancer, and continue on your path. You know where the true value lies. Depth, understanding and connection will take you further than a little superficial sparkle. Glitter might catch the light and be the first thing you notice, but it doesn't hold the attention for long.

Your emotions are close to the surface again today Cancer, possibly so close that you can see physical manifestations of stress or strain. Take some dedicated time for yourself, and perhaps even seek the advice of a specialist if this problem seems too weighty to lift alone.

Finally, it feels as though things are starting to play your way again Cancer, with your supporters close by and the challenges seemingly well-matched to your strengths. Enjoy this one – it seems made for you.

You have so much going for
you Cancer, and it's the little things
stacking up that will make the big
difference, rather than one or two
knock-out shots. You've done
the groundwork well; you can be
confident in your abilities now.

With so much movement at the
moment, it's important to stay alert
and on top of all the change and flux.
Even though you are a water sign, and
well used to going with the flow,
finding yourself swept away at the
moment would be far from ideal.

Staying in control might seem difficult right now, but if you narrow your territory even slightly, so you have less responsibility, it will make this infinitely easier.

Your goals are in sight, so stay focused. Don't be distracted by the proximity of the win; it could still all go wrong if you celebrate too soon.

It is essential you are firm
and insistent if there is something
particularly important you need dealt
with right now Cancer. Do not allow
anyone to fob you off just because
they might perceive the task as
difficult or troublesome. It won't
go away as easily as that.

Keep your loved ones in mind Cancer – with so much going on, and so many things to think about and distract you, it can sometimes be easy to forget what is really important.

Being serious is not at all the same as being confrontational, far from it. If someone is taking offence at your insistence that they pay attention, it may be that their own lack of ability (or lack of self-awareness) is more to blame than anything you have done.

Dedication and commitment
to doing a decent job is part of your
Cancer character, but so are extreme
sensitivity and, inevitably, a strongly
self-protective streak. If you are feeling
defensive at the moment, think about
whether there might be a way you
could achieve more alone.

Highly intuitive, even to the
point of what some might call psychic,
you are also aware that managing your
emotions and responses is your own
responsibility and no one else's. Do
not allow yourself to be cornered or
injured by the feelings of others;
retreat inside that crab shell and let
anything extraneous simply
slide right past you.

Feeling indecisive Cancer?
Don't let it stop you moving forwards
– there is more than one right answer,
so it follows that you would be
perfectly justified in choosing
more than one option.

Noticing and accepting are key
in the quest to get along peacefully
together; remember that Cancer,
especially when everything feels
confused or chaotic. Your role is
not to assess, alter or educate,
you need only observe.

The classic water sign, Cancer,
you are happiest and most in tune
when you go with the flow... but
actually doing it is often not as easy
as simply saying it. Practicing allowing
and letting go is an ongoing and
daily commitment.

Time to expand your horizons Cancer – there is more than one way to get this done, and adventure can be part of the path you choose. Remember, journeys may take many forms – this time it might not be obvious at first that this is what's on offer.

Building in time for fun is
important for you Cancer – don't let
the seriousness of life overwhelm you
to the point you forget to enjoy it.
There is lightness and love to be
tasted as well.

If calm eludes you at the moment
and your brain is fizzing with ideas and
possibilities: embrace it. This is a
positive lift in your energies and a sign
that everything is realigning and your
creativity is reasserting itself. Allow
yourself the room you need to
spread your wings.

Gathering facts and information
is a vital task at the moment Cancer;
there will be choices to be made and
going the right way depends on a
complete and full understanding of
what each option entails. Gather
before you progress.

Maintain that focus on thinking before you act Cancer – it's generally a more effective way to run things. Even if your intuition is messaging you non-stop, pause to consider what it really means before you take things further.

Even if others would have
you rush into action or decision, do
not allow yourself to be swept along
on their panicky wave Cancer. If you
feel that more thinking time would be
of greater benefit than an immediate,
ill-thought-through reaction,
speak up and say so.

Things might not be exactly
as they seem right now Cancer.
Perhaps you are carrying a weight you
would like to set down but can't see
where to place it? Be patient and
watch for the next surge of energy
and opportunity.

Frustration is not an unfamiliar
feeling, but the urge to get on with
things combined with not knowing
which way to go is also confusing.
Don't tie yourself in knots then trip
over your own ropes Cancer. Distract
yourself with something easy until
the way ahead is clearer.

It's important to carve out some
alone time, whatever way you can
manage it Cancer. Maintaining that
all-important momentum will only be
possible if you take the time you need
to recharge now and then.

Balance and harmony are particularly vital for you Cancer, and when you feel pulled too far in any particular direction it can really topple your focus. Take time to come back to the centre and check in with yourself.

Understanding what others
are on about can sometimes prove
a stumbling block Cancer, if only
because their thought processes and
logic (or lack of it) can seem so
unnecessarily complicated. Don't let
this infuriate you, instead choose to be
amused by your differences.

Now is a good time to refocus on yourself as an individual Cancer; time to explore your strengths and hopes for your own future.

Interrogating the reasons and motivations of others won't lead you anywhere right now Cancer, you will simply end up scuttling around in a time-wasting, tail-chasing circle. They will learn their own lessons in their own time... or perhaps not. Really, it's not your problem.

Indecision is not necessarily a negative Cancer; it might be that the universe is slowing you down on purpose, asking you to take a closer look before you commit.

Confronted with an issue that feels like a brick wall, your tendency might well be to inspect it for a long while, looking for a crack, or a ladder, or a hidden door – anything that will help you find a way through. Far better to distract yourself with something else Cancer, and perhaps come back to this one later. It might not feel quite so insurmountable then.

Resist the urge to be at the centre
of the action right now Cancer;
move off to the sidelines and let
everyone find their own way. Wait
patiently and balance will be restored.

Flexibility and sideways thinking are
two of your particularly valuable gifts
Cancer. You seem to know instinctively
how to find your way around difficult
people and how to deal with sticky
situations. Be willing and generous in
sharing that wisdom with others,
but only if they request it.

Agreeing with someone who disagrees with you can be a delicate balancing act Cancer, but it might be essential if you are attempting to find common ground with a stubborn or contrary sort of person. Don't take it all to heart; instead, think what a good story it will make later on and laugh it off.

Harmony is always a major goal for you Cancer, and being in sync with those around you is a true reward. Accepting differences rather than trying to change them is a major step in the right direction.

Connecting with others is vital
for your own growth Cancer; unless
you can find the space to grow into
and the support to do it, you
may become stuck.

Don't be afraid to give an honest opinion but do take care to deliver it in the gentlest way possible. You never know who might be listening or how it might be subsequently reported.

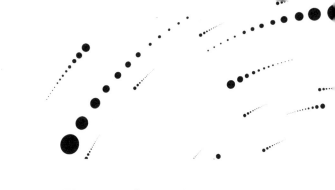

Time to plunge into your feelings and explore what your heart truly wants Cancer. It might seem all too much right now but be honest with yourself about your desired destination. There are hidden possibilities.

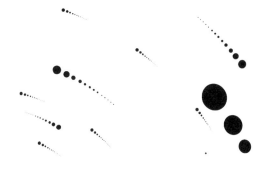

Delving into your emotions
and answering tough questions
will inevitably bring difficult feelings
to the fore. It's all part of the
process Cancer.

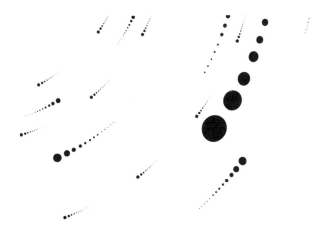

Communication and connection
are key for Cancer – without them,
it can feel a little like you are unable to
get a foothold, constantly trying to
stay upright on shifting sands. But
take a pause on trying to express
yourself for once and allow some
space for others to approach
you instead.

If you have been in a holding
pattern lately, now is the time to
set yourself back on course Cancer.
Use your intuition to set your
coordinates for a suitably
soulful destination, then power
up that engine and get moving.

Demanding attention will never get you what you want Cancer, even if you feel you are perfectly justified in doing so after all the effort you have put in. Regardless, if security is what you're looking for then you need to know others will meet you halfway.
It's not up to you to chase.

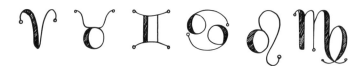

Your charm and natural
instincts will always lead you in
the right direction, and ultimately the
best people for you will come to you.
Resist the urge to compare your
situation and status with those of
others; you cannot know what price
they truly pay for what they have.
Run your own race.

While you love company, staying grounded and secure within your own self-knowledge is one of your most attractive traits Cancer. You are satisfied and happy in your own company, and this is truly a gift. Enjoy it when you can because, ironically, it is also one of the traits that makes others eager to be around you.

Wait and see what shows up
Cancer, resist that push to make things
happen and instead watch for what
the universe sends. The outcome will
be better this way.

Don't allow others to sap your emotional energy Cancer. Someone as empathetic as you runs the risk of burn-out if you fail to be firm about your boundaries. Be careful about the ways you engage and how much of yourself you give. You cannot save everyone.

Taking risks isn't really your
bag Cancer, but now and again,
when you choose your timing carefully
and go for broke, it can pay off. Now
looks like it might be one of those
times, so choose courage and open
yourself up to possibility.

Time to take that gamble you have been weighing up Cancer... be bold and stay in the moment. You will need to keep your eyes open if you are to recognize that opportunity when it finally presents itself.

Keep your contacts book open
Cancer; connections and colleagues
might be able to help you right now.
You don't ask for support very often,
but if your heart is set on a particular
goal you may need to borrow some
maps and ask for directions.

Creativity is never in short supply for you Cancer, and with the moon in charge you get an extra boost virtually every day. Open your mind to what this might mean – whether problem-solving, finding the roots of things, understanding others or growing something from virtually nothing – it's all within your creative power. Use it wisely.

Stay within your budget Cancer, both literally and metaphorically. There is no point bankrupting yourself in order to simply take a shot or emulate someone else's style or approach. Finding more meaningful ways to enrich your life will ultimately be more worthwhile.

While you are so focused
on thinking about other people,
it won't be possible to put your
energies into assessing your own
situation Cancer. Maybe, for the
time being, that is for the best.

Your connections are vital to you
Cancer, but be careful not to risk
losing your sense of self within your
experience of belonging and affiliation.

Repaying favours and debts owed
should be a priority right now Cancer
– don't leave any loose ends hanging if
you can tie them off instead.

Putting so much time and
energy into supporting your friends
and loved ones is admirable Cancer,
but do ensure a balance between
caring for others and looking
after your own interests.

Something that looks like it is flowing super-smoothly may not be at all as it seems Cancer. Keep an eye out for potential glitches or points where the threads might catch and snag.

Your Cancer brain loves a challenge and solving problems is a particular joy for you. If you find yourself in the middle of a bit of chaos, roll up your sleeves and enjoy sorting it all out.

Joining with others to achieve a resolution will bring particular rewards right now Cancer. Even if you feel you could cope with this one alone, take some time to glean the thoughts of those around you. You may be surprised by different, perhaps even better, perspectives and options you hadn't considered.

Changes don't automatically mean improvements Cancer; be careful not to mistake simply shifting sideways for stepping up.

Anything you do often enough will eventually become routine, even habit, Cancer. No matter how strange and unfamiliar new things might seem, you will get used to them if you stick with them.

Give everything time to settle,
especially if a recent period of
adjustment has been particularly
tumultuous. Listen to your intuition
and take things one step at a time.

Perhaps your social circle is feeling a little tight now Cancer... you might just need a change of scenery. Mix things up a bit.

Stretching outside your comfort zone will be of enormous benefit to everybody right now Cancer – just make sure you don't abandon your existing responsibilities.